THE SIGHT OF HELL

BY THE
REV. JOHN FURNISS C.SS.R

New York

Published by Curious Publications
101 W. 23rd St. #318
New York, NY 10011
curiouspublications.com

Copyright © 2020

Cover image: Hell, from *Hortus deliciarum,* by Herrad of Landsberg, 1180.
(Public domain - Wikimedia Commons)

Frontispiece: The hellmouth, set design from "Il Pomo D'Oro," 1688.
(Metropolitan Museum of Art / CC0 - Wikimedia Commons)

Back cover image: *Hours of Catherine of Cleves,* by the Master of Catherine of Cleves, circa 1440. (Morgan Library & Museum, Public domain / Wikimedia Commons)

This edition of *The Sight of Hell* was published in 1874 by
James Duffy & Co., Ltd.

ISBN-13: 978-0-9862393-9-7

Printed and bound in the United States of America.

A NOTE ON THE TEXT

The Sight of Hell was written "for children and young persons" by the Reverend John Furniss in 1861, however this reprint is from an 1874 publication. The images of Hell in the pages that follow have all been added—Furniss's original booklet left everything to his readers' imaginations.

In 1914, *The Month* described the reverend as "a pious and devoted priest on the English mission, noted for his zeal in promoting religious education." Read any sentence this pious man wrote and you may find that more severe terms would be better suited in characterizing him. Watch your language though—you wouldn't want to find yourself burning in the middle of the earth until the red-hot fiery heat goes into your brain and melts it.

The Sight of Hell, as you'll notice from the image of the 1874 cover included within, is the tenth book in Furniss's series, which also boasts *The House of Death* and *The Book of the Dying*. According to *The Irish Ecclesiastical Record* from 1896, the publisher sold "upwards of four million copies of his booklets," meaning at least four million young people were thoroughly terrorized and scared straight.

Now, before you journey into the depths of Hell that reside between these covers, enjoy a few short reviews of Furniss's work. They're exclusive to this edition.

Happy reading. And please, remember not to sin, or a devil may be striking you "every minute for ever and ever, without ever stopping."

Nineteenth-Century Reviews of *The Sight of Hell*.

"All About Hell"
(*The Israelite*, Dec 14, 1866)

One Rev. J. Furniss wrote a book called "The Sight of Hell," which affords another striking evidence, that not all fools are dead; because the author must certainly believe that some are left to purchase his book.

His book is but a pamphlet, but it is stuffed with as many horrors as if an encyclopedia had been devoted to the subject; and it is after this fashion that children belonging to the Church of which Mr. Furniss is a zealous teacher, are encouraged to have their trust in a God who is, before all things, a God of Love. Children are informed that Hell is four thousand miles from the surface of the earth, that the fair saint, St. Frances, has been taken over the interior of that place of torment by the angel Gabriel; and from her account and that of other witnesses, living children have an opportunity of knowing whither they are sure to go, and what they are certain to suffer, for ever and ever, for the smallest mortal crime committed in the flesh. Let us here remark, parenthetically, that we have no opinion to offer touching the theological character of the book. We take it as a literary and social illustration of what is now being written, and of the influences it is expected to have on a rising generation. We commit all besides to the fair judgment of our readers.

Mr. Furniss then informs the young that Hell is boundless, its plain is of red-hot iron, its atmosphere a fog of fire, its rivers fathomless streams of soothing pitch and sulphur. Take the least spark from Hell (he says); throw it into the ocean, and in a moment it will dry up all the waters and set the whole world in a blaze. The music of Hell is not that of the spheres, but made up of shrieks that never subside, and unnatural sounds from the condemned, who roar like lions, hiss like serpents, howl like dogs, and wail like dragons. There is a rushing thunder us of cataracts of water, but little children are reminded that there is no water in Satan's glory kingdom. What sounds like the fall thereof are the torrents of scalding tears filling without any cessation from millions of millions of eyes! The young, too, are further sickened by the assurance that if a body could be snatched for a moment from Hell, and laid upon the earth, the stencil would be so overwhelming, that everything would wither and die. Then the little ones are further scared by the information that millions of fiends are daily dispatched from the Bottomless Pit especially to tempt children to sin, and that the fiends are well beaten when they return home at night if they have been unsuccessful in destroying the souls of children throughout the day. As for the awful subject of judgment, these little ones again are told that their offending souls will be dragged in chains before Satan's judgment seat, that he is their judge—and a judge without mercy!

"A Pleasant Book for Children"
(*Daily Record*, April 24, 1872)

[This] charming little book entitled "The Sight of Hell," by the Rev. Father Furniss, C.SS.R., is printed "permissu superiorum" and is recommended to be used along with the Catechism in Sunday schools as a part of a course of religious instructions. It is one of a series of "Books for Children and Young Persons." From the following extract it will be seen that the work is not of an inspiring character. ... "Little children, if you go to hell there will be a devil at your side to strike you. He will go on striking you every minute for ever and ever without stopping." ...

They also have a peep at a baby in a red-hot oven: "Hear how it screams to come out! See how it turns and twists itself about in the fire! It beats its head against the roof of the oven. It stamps its little feet against the floor of the oven—You can see on the face of all in hell—despair, desperate and horrible."

What a dear, nice, excellent, tender teacher of little children this Father Furnace must make!

"Boiled Boys and Roasted Babies"
(*Republican Banner*, April 14, 1872)

... With such a friend as Mr. Furniss for preceptor, children with whom he labors might not, perhaps, see the full horrors of such scenes as these, and might prefer becoming "boiling boys" and girls with "burning bonnets" to remaining long in his amiable society.

BOOKS FOR CHILDREN, AND YOUNG PERSONS.

BOOK X.

THE SIGHT OF HELL.

BY THE

REV. J. FURNISS, C.SS.R.

PERMISSU SUPERIORUM.

Dublin:
JAMES DUFFY AND CO., Ltd.,
38 WESTMORELAND STREET.

PRICE ONE PENNY.

CONTENTS

Section	Page
I. — Where is Hell—The Earth Opening	13
II. — The Burning Mountain	14
III. — How far it is to Hell	15
IV. — The Gates of Hell	15
V. — The first Look into Hell	17
VI. — Fire	17
VII. — Darkness	18
VIII. — Smoke	19
IX. — Terrific Noise	21
X. — A River	21
XI. — The Smell of Death	22
XII. — The Devil	23
XIII. — What the Devil does in Hell—Temptation	24
XIV. — Judgment	25
XV. — A Soul coming into Hell	25
XVI. — The Soul before Satan	26
XVII. — The everlasting Dwelling Place of the Soul	26
XVIII. — The Striking Devil	27
XIX. — The Mocking Devil	30

Section	Page
XX. — A Bed of Fire	31
XXI. — Worms	31
XXII. — Fright	32
XXIII. — The Pain of Loss	33
XXIV. — The Dungeons of Hell — The First Dungeon — A Dress Of Fire	34
XXV. — Second Dungeon — The Deep Pit	35
XXVI. — Third Dungeon — The Red-Hot Floor	36
XXVII. — Fourth Dungeon — The Boiling Kettle	38
XXVIII. — Fifth Dungeon — The Red-Hot Oven. Sixth Dungeon — A Voice	38
XXIX. — Hunger, The Drunkard	40
XXX. — No Peace — Two Vipers — A Picture of Hell	41
XXXI. — Eternity — The Question — A Measure — A Bird	43
XXXII. — Tears — Sand — Dots	44
XXXIII. — What are they Doing? — What o'clock? — The Dismal Sound	45
XXXIV. — Too Late! — The Prayer of a Lost Soul — The Answer of Jesus Christ	46
XXXV. — Despair — The Knife	49
XXXVI. — The Vision of St. Teresa — A Pair of Scales — Break the Egg — The Devil's Trap	51
XXXVII. — The Vision in Ven. Bede	54

THE SIGHT OF HELL

I. WHERE IS HELL?

Ps. lxii.—*"They shall go into the lower parts of the Earth."*

EVERY little child knows that God will reward the good in Heaven and punish the wicked in Hell. Where, then, is Hell? Is Hell above or below? Is it on the earth, or in the earth, or below the earth?

It seems likely that Hell is in the middle of the earth. Almighty God has said that *"He will turn the wicked into the bowels of the earth."*—Ecclus. xvii.

THE EARTH OPENING.

In the days of the Jews, there were three very wicked men. Their names were Core, Dathan, and Abiron. They were very disobedient to the priests. God had made Moses master over all the people. He told Moses that He was going to punish the wicked men. Moses went and told the people to come away from the wicked men. The people came away. Then Moses said to them: "By this you shall know that God has sent me. If these wicked men die like other men, then do not believe me; but if the earth open, and swallow them, and they go down alive into hell, then you shall know that they are wicked."

As soon as Moses had done speaking, the earth broke open under the feet of the wicked men. It drew them in with all they had, and they went down alive into Hell.

Then the earth closed up over them again.—Numb. xvi. The same thing happened another time, as you will see.

II. THE BURNING MOUNTAIN.

St. Gregory says, "There was a very wicked and cruel king. His name was Theodoric. He lived in a town called Ravenna. At the same time there was a holy Pope called John, living in Rome. One day this holy Pope went to the town where Theodoric the cruel king was living. When Theodoric heard that the Pope was come, he had him put in prison. He gave him very little to eat, and was very cruel to him. In a few days the good Pope died in the prison. Very soon after Theodoric had killed the Pope, he killed another good man called Symmachus. Soon after this the cruel king Theodoric died himself. You will see how God punished him.

"There is a little island called Stromboli, with water all round it. On this island there is a great mountain. Fire is often seen coming out of the top of this mountain.

"At that time there was a holy hermit living on the island in a little cell or room. On the night that cruel king, Theodoric, died, it happened that the hermit was looking out of the window. He saw three persons near the top of the fiery mountain. They were persons who were dead. But he had seen them all before. So he knew who they were. There was Theodoric, the cruel king, who had died that night. The other two were Pope John and Symmachus, who had been unjustly killed by Theodoric. He saw that Theodoric was in the middle betwixt the other two. When they came to that place where the fire was coming out, he saw Theodoric leave the other two, and go down into the fiery mountain. So," says Saint Gregory, "those who had seen the cruel king's injustice saw also his punishment."

III. HOW FAR IT IS TO HELL.

WE know how far it is to the middle of the Earth. It is just four thousand miles. So if Hell is in the middle of the Earth, it is four thousand miles to the horrible prison of Hell.

It is time now to do what St. Augustine bids us. He says—"Let us go down to Hell while we live, that we may not have to go down to Hell when we die." If we go and look at that Terrible Prison, where those who commit mortal sin are punished, we shall be afraid to commit mortal sin. If we do not commit mortal sin, we shall not go to Hell.

IV. THE GATES OF HELL.

Matt. xvi.—*"The Gates of Hell shall not prevail against the Church."*

St. Frances of Rome lived a very holy life. Many times she saw with her eyes her Angel Guardian at her side. It pleased the Almighty God to let her see many other wonderful things.—*Brev. Rom.* One afternoon the Angel Gabriel came to take her to see Hell. She went with him and saw that terrible place. Let us follow in her footsteps, that we may see in spirit the wonderful things which she saw. Our journey is through the deep dark places under the earth. Now we will set off. We pass through hundreds and hundreds of miles of darkness. Now we are coming near the terrible place. See, there are the gates of Hell! When St. Frances came to the gates of Hell, she read on them these words written in letters of fire—"This is Hell, where there is neither rest, nor consolation, nor hope." Look, then, at those tremendous gates in front of you. How large they are. Measure, if you can, the length and breadth, the height and depth of the terrible gates. Isa. v.—"Therefore hath Hell *opened her mouth without any bound.* Their strong ones, and their people, and their glorious ones go down into it." See also the vast thickness, the tremendous strength of those gates. In a prison on earth, there are not, perhaps, more than two or three hundred prisoners; still the gates of a prison are made most strong with iron, and with bars, and with bolts, and with locks, for fear the prisoners should break down the gates and get away. Do not wonder, then, at the immense strength of the Gates of Hell. In Hell there are not two or three hundred prisoners only. Millions on millions are shut up there. They are tormented with the most frightful pains. These dreadful pains make them furious. Their fury gives them strength, such as we never saw. We read of a man who had the fury of Hell in him. He was so strong that he could easily break in pieces great chains of iron.—Mark v. The vast multitudes in Hell, strong in their fury and despair, rush forward like the waves of the sea. They dash themselves up against the gates of Hell to break them in pieces. This is the reason why those gates are so strong. No hand of man could make such gates. Jesus Christ said that the Gates of Hell should not prevail against His Church, because in Hell there is nothing stronger than its gates.

Do you hear that growling thunder rolling from one end of Hell to the other. The Gates of Hell are opening.

V. THE FIRST LOOK INTO HELL.

WHEN the Gates of Hell had been opened, St. Frances with her angel went forward. She stood on the edge of the abyss. She saw a sight so terrible that it cannot be told. She saw that the size of Hell was immense. Neither in height, nor in depth, nor in length nor in breadth, could she see any end of it. Isa. xxxiv.—*"None shall ever pass through it."* She saw that Hell was divided into three immense places. These three places were at a great distance from one another. There was an upper Hell, and a middle Hell, and a lower Hell. Wisd. xvii.—*"Night came upon them from the lowest and deepest Hell."* She saw that in the upper Hell, the torments were very grievous. In the middle Hell they were still more terrible. In the lowest Hell the torments were above all understanding. When she had looked into this terrible place, her blood was frozen with fright!

VI. FIRE.

NOW look into Hell and see what she saw. Look at the floor of Hell. It is red-hot like red-hot iron. Streams of burning pitch and sulphur run through it.—Isa. xxxiv. The floor blazes up to the roof. Look at the walls, the enormous stones are red-hot; sparks of fire are always falling down from them. Lift up your eyes to the roof of Hell; it is like a sheet of blazing fire. Sometimes when you get up on a winter's morning, you see the country filled with a great thick fog. Hell is filled with a fog of fire. In some parts of the world torrents of rain come down which sweep away trees and houses. In Hell torrents, not of rain, but of fire and brimstone, are rained down. Ps. x—*"The Lord shall rain down on sinners fire and brim-*

stone." Storms of hailstones come down on the earth and break the windows in pieces. But in Hell the hailstones are thunderbolts, red-hot balls of fire. Job. xli.—*"God shall send thunderbolts against him."* See that great whirlwind of fire sweeping across Hell. *"Storms of winds shall be the portion of their cup."*—Ps. x. Look how floods of fire roll themselves through Hell like the waves of the sea. The wicked are sunk down and buried in that fiery sea of destruction and perdition.—1 Tim. vi. You may have seen a house on fire. But you never saw a house made of fire. Hell is a house made of fire. The fire of Hell burns the devils who are spirits, for it was prepared for them.— Matt. xxv. So it will burn the soul as well as the body. Take a spark out of the kitchen fire, throw it into the sea, and it will go out. Take a little spark out of Hell less than a pin-head, throw it into the ocean, it will not go out. In one moment it would dry up all the waters of the ocean, and set the whole world in a blaze. Wisd. xvi.—*"The fire above its power, burnt in the midst of water."* Set a house or town on fire. Perhaps the fire may burn for a week, or a month, but it will go out at last. But the fire of Hell will never go out: it will burn for ever. It is *unquenchable fire.*— Matt. iv. St. Teresa says, that the fire on the earth is only a *picture* of the fire of Hell. Fire on earth gives light. But it is not so in Hell. In Hell the fire is dark.

VII. — DARKNESS.

Isa. xxi.—*"Watchman, what of the night? The watchman said: The night cometh."*

The watchman did not say the nights are coming, but only the night. He said so, because in Hell there is only one night, one eternal night, one everlasting night.

The fire in Hell burns, but gives no light. Wisd. ii.—*"No power of fire could give them light."* No stray sunbeam, no wandering ray of starlight ever creeps into the darkness of Hell. All is darkness — thick, black, heavy, pitchy, aching darkness. It is not darkness like ours, which is only *an image of the darkness to come.*—Wisd. xviii. This darkness is thicker than the darkness of the land of Egypt which could be touched with the hand. *"So the wicked in Hell will never see light."*—Ps. xlviii. This darkness is made worse by the smoke of Hell.

VIII. SMOKE.

Apoc. xvi.—*"The smoke of their torments shall go up for ever and ever."*

Stop up that chimney where the fire is burning. In half an hour the room will be full of smoke, so that you cannot stay there. The great fires of Hell have been smoking now for nearly six thousand years. They will go on smoking for ever. There is no chimney to take this smoke off; there is no wind to blow it away. See those great, black, heavy sulphurous clouds rising up every moment from the dark fires. They rise up till the roof or Hell stops them. The roof drives them back again. Slowly they go down into the abyss of Hell. There they are joined by more dark clouds of smoke leaving the fires. So Hell is filled with sulphur and smoke, in which no one on earth could breathe or live. How then do they live in Hell? In Hell they must live, but they are stifled and choked each moment, as if they were dying. Now listen!

Entrance to Hell, by Theodoor Galle, 1603.
(Rijksmuseum / CC0 - Wikimedia Commons)

IX. TERRIFIC NOISE.

Exodus xi.—*"There shall be a great cry such as hath not been heard before."*

You have heard, perhaps, a horrible scream in the dead of night. You may have heard the last shriek of a drowning man, before he went down into his watery grave. You may have been shocked in passing a madhouse, to hear the wild shout of a madman. Your heart may have trembled when you heard the roar of a lion in the desert or the hissing of a deadly serpent in the bushes.

But listen now—listen to the tremendous, the horrible uproar of millions and millions and millions of tormented creatures mad with the fury of Hell. Oh, the screams of fear, the groanings of horror, the yells of rage, the cries of pain, the shouts of agony, the shrieks of despair from millions on millions. There you hear them roaring like lions, hissing like serpents, howling like dogs, and wailing like dragons. There you hear the gnashing of teeth and the fearful blasphemies of the devils. Above all, you hear the roaring of the thunders of God's anger, which shakes Hell to its foundations. But there is another sound!

X. A RIVER.

Isa. xxii.—*"It is the day of slaughter and of treading down, and of weeping to the Lord the God of hosts."*

There is in Hell a sound like that of many waters. It is as if all the rivers and oceans of the world were pouring themselves with a great splash down on the floor of Hell. Is it then really the sound of waters? It is. Are the rivers and oceans of the earth pouring themselves into Hell. No. What is it then? It is the sound of oceans of tears running down from countless millions of eyes. They cry night and day. They cry for ever and ever. They cry because the sulphurous smoke torments their eyes. They cry because they are in darkness. They cry because they have lost the beautiful heaven. They cry because the sharp fire burns them.

Little child, it is better to cry one tear of repentance now than to cry millions of tears in Hell. But what is that dreadful sickening smell?

XI. THE SMELL OF DEATH.

Joel ii.—*"His stench shall ascend, and his rottenness shall go up."*

There are some diseases so bad, such as cancers and ulcers, that people cannot bear to breathe the air in the house where they are. There is something worse. It is the smell of death coming from a dead body lying in the grave. The dead body of Lazarus had been in the grave only four days. Yet Martha his sister could not bear that it should be taken out again. But what is the smell of death in Hell. St. Bonaventure says that if one single body was taken out of Hell and laid on the earth, in that same moment every living creature on the earth would sicken and die. Such is the smell of death from one body in Hell. What then will be the smell of death from countless millions and millions of bodies laid in Hell like sheep?—Ps. How will the horrible smell of all these bodies be, after it has been getting worse and worse every moment for ten thousand years? Isa. lxvi.—"They shall go out and see the carcasses of the men that have transgressed against Me. They shall be a loathsome sight to all flesh."

THE DEVIL

Now let us enter into Hell and see the tremendous torments prepared for the wicked.

XII. THE DEVIL.

Apoc. XX.— *"An angel laid hold on the old serpent, which is the devil and Satan, and bound him, and cast him into the bottomless pit, and shut him up."*

Our journey lies across that great sea of fire. We must go on till we come to the middle of Hell. There we shall see the most horrible sight that ever was or will be—the great devil chained down in the middle of Hell. We will set off on our journey. Now we are coming near the dwelling-place of Satan. The darkness gets thicker. You see a great number of devils moving about in the thick darkness. They come to get the orders of their great chief. Already you hear the rattling of the tremendous chains of the great monster! See I there he is—the most horrible and abominable of all monsters, the devil.

His size is immense! Isa. viii.—*"He shall fill the length of the land."* St. Frances saw him. He was sitting on a long beam which passed through the middle of Hell. His feet went down into the lowest depths of Hell. They rested on the floor of Hell. They were fastened with great, heavy iron chains. These chains were fixed to an immense ring in the floor. His hands were chained up to the roof. One of his hands was turned up against Heaven to blaspheme God and the saints who dwell there.—Apoc. xiii. His other hand was stretched out, pointing to the lowest Hell! His tremendous and horrible head was raised up on high, and touched the roof. From his head came two immense horns. Apoc. xiii.—*"I saw another beast having two horns."* From each horn smaller horns without number branched out, which like chimneys sent out fire and smoke. His enormous mouth was wide open. Out of it there was running a river of fire, which gave no light, but a most abominable smell. Job xli.—*"Flame Cometh out of his mouth."* Round his neck was a collar of red-hot iron. A burning chain tied him round the middle. The ugliness of his face was such, that no man or devil could bear it. It was the most deformed, horrible, frightful thing that ever was or will be. His great fierce eyes were filled with pride, and anger, and rage, and spite, and blood, and fire, and savage cruelty. There was something else in those eyes for which there is no name, but it made those on whom the devil's eyes were fixed tremble and shake as if they were dying. One of the Saints who saw the devil said she would rather be burnt for a thousand years than look at the devil for one moment!

XIII. WHAT THE DEVIL DOES IN HELL.

1. TEMPTATION.

Job xli.—*"He beholdeth every high thing, he is king over all the children of pride."*

As the devil is king of Hell, he does two things. First, he gives his orders to the other devils about tempting people in the world. Without his leave, no one in Hell can stir hand or foot. Millions and millions of devils are always round him waiting for his orders. Every day he sends wicked spirits, whose numbers cannot be counted, into Europe, Asia, Africa, America, into every country, and town, and village, and house, and to every human creature. He sends them for temptation and the ruin of souls. He tells each devil, whom he must tempt, what he must do, and when he must come back. St. Frances saw that when these devils came back, if they had not made people commit sin, they were cruelly beaten. When a child is tempted, how little it thinks that the temptation has been got ready in Hell, that there is a devil at its side who has brought the temptation, and this devil is breathing the temptation into its heart, and trying to make it do what the bad company wants it to do.

XIV. 2. JUDGMENT.

As the devil is king of Hell, he is also judge. When a soul comes into Hell, condemned by the judgment of God, he executes the judgment. He fixes whereabouts in Hell the soul is to be, how it is to be tormented, and what devils are to torment it. In a moment you will see his judgment on a soul.

XV. A SOUL COMING INTO HELL.

ST. Frances saw souls coming into Hell, after they had been condemned by the judgment of God. They came with letters of fire written on their foreheads. Apoc. xii.—*"He shall make all, both little and great, have a character on their forehead."* On their foreheads were written the names of the sins for which they had been condemned in Hell. *Blaspheming, or impurity, or stealing, or drunkenness, or not hearing Mass on Sundays, or not going to the Sacraments on* Sunday, etc. As soon as any of these souls came to the gates of Hell, the devils went and seized hold of it. Job xx.—*"The terrible ones shall go and come down upon him."* But what sort of devils took hold of these souls? The prophet Daniel saw one of them. He says, chap. vii. —"I beheld, in a vision by night, a beast, terrible, and wonderful, and exceeding strong. It had great iron teeth, eating and breaking in pieces, and treading down the rest with its teeth." How do the devils take hold of these souls? As the lions in Babylon took hold of those who were thrown into their den.

When the people were thrown over the wall into the den, the lions opened their mouths and roared and caught the people in their mouths and crushed them, even before they had fallen to the ground. So is a soul received by the devil when it comes to Hell.

XVI. THE SOUL BEFORE SATAN.

The devils carry away the soul which has just come into Hell. They bear it through the flames. Now they have set it down in front of the great chained monster, to be judged by him who has no mercy. Oh, that terrible face of the devil! Oh, the fright, the shivering, the freezing, the deadly horror of that soul at the first sight of the great devil. Now the devil opens his mouth. He gives out the tremendous sentence on the soul. All hear the sentence, and Hell rings with shouts of spiteful joy and mockeries at the unfortunate soul.

XVII. THE EVERLASTING DWELLING-PLACE OF THE SOUL.

As soon as the sentence is given, the soul is snatched away and hurried to that place which is to be its home for ever and ever! Crowds of hideous devils have met together. With cries of spiteful joy they receive the soul. Isa. xxxiv.—*"Demons and monsters shall meet. The hairy ones shall cry out to one another."* See how these devils receive the soul in this time of destruction. Ecclus. xxxix.—"In the time of destruction, they shall pour out their force. The teeth of serpents, and beasts, and scorpions, the sword taking vengeance on the ungodly unto destruction."

Immediately the soul is thrust by the devils into that prison which is to be its dwelling-place for evermore. The prison of each soul is different according to its sins.

"St. Teresa found herself squeezed into a hole or chest in the wall. Here the walls, which were most terrible, seemed to close upon her and strangle her. She found her soul burning in a most horrible fire. It seemed as if some one was always tearing her soul in pieces, or rather as if the soul was always tearing itself in pieces. It was impossible to sit or lie down, for there was no room." As soon as the soul is fixed in its place, it finds two devils, one on each side of it. *"There art spirits created for vengeance, and in their fury they lay on grievous torments."*—Ecclus. xxxix. St. Frances saw them. One of them is called the striking devil, the other the mocking devil.

XVIII. THE STRIKING DEVIL.

Prov. xix.—*"Striking hammers are prepared for the bodies of sinners."*

If you want to know what sort of a stroke the devil can give, hear how he struck Job. Chap. ii—"Satan went forth from the presence of the Lord, and *struck* Job with a grievous ulcer from the sole of his foot to the top of his head. Then Job took a tile and scraped off the corrupt matter, sitting on a dung-hill. Now when Job's friends heard all the evil that had come upon him, they came to him. For they had made an appointment to come together and visit and comfort him. And when they had lifted up their eyes afar off they did not know him. And crying they wept and sprinkled dust on their heads. And they sat down with him on the ground for seven days and seven nights. And no one spoke a word to him, for they saw that his grief was very great."

The devil gave Job one stroke, only one stroke. That one stroke was so terrible, that it covered all his body with sores and ulcers. That one stroke made Job look so frightful, that his friends did not know him again. That one stroke was so terrible, that for seven days and seven nights his friends did not speak a word, but sat crying, and wondering, and thinking what a terrible stroke the devil can give.

Little child, if you go to Hell, there will be a devil at your side to strike you. He will go on striking you every minute for ever and ever, without ever stopping. The first stroke will make your body as bad as the body of Job, covered from head to foot with sores and ulcers. The second stroke will make your body twice as bad as the body of Job. The third stroke will make your body three times as bad as the body of Job. The fourth stroke will make your body four times as bad as the body of Job. How then will your body be, after the devil has been striking it every moment for a hundred million of years without stopping?

But there was one good thing for Job. When the devil had struck Job, his friends came to visit and comfort him, and when they saw him they cried. But when the devil is striking you in Hell, there will be no one to come and visit and comfort you, and cry with you. Neither father, nor mother, nor brother, nor sister, nor friend will ever come to cry with you. Lam. i.—"Weeping she hath wept in the night, and the tears are on her cheeks, because there is none to comfort her amongst all them

An angel unlocking the Door of Hell, circa 12th century.
(British Library / CC0 - Wikimedia Commons)

that were dear to her." Little child, it is a bad bargain to make with the devil, to commit a mortal sin, and then to be beaten for ever for it.

XIX. THE MOCKING DEVIL.

Hab. ii.—*"Shall they not take up a parable against him, a dark speech concerning him?"*

St. Frances saw that on the other side of the soul there was another devil to mock at and reproach it. Hear what mockeries he said to it. "Remember," he said, "remember where you are and where you will be for ever: how short the sin was, how long the punishment. It is your own fault; when you committed that mortal sin you knew how you would be punished. What a good bargain you made to take the pains of eternity in exchange for the sin of a day, an hour, a moment. You cry now for your sin, but your crying comes too late. You liked bad company, you will find bad company enough here. Your father was a drunkard and showed you the way to the public-house; he is still a drunkard, look at him over there drinking red-hot fire. You were too idle to go to Mass on Sundays, be as idle as you like now, for there is no Mass to go to. You disobeyed your father, but you dare not disobey him who is your father in Hell. Look at him, that great chained monster; disobey him if you dare."

St. Frances saw that these mockeries put the soul into such dreadful despair that it burst out into the most frightful howlings and blasphemies.

But it is time for us now to see where the sinner has been put—his everlasting dwelling-place.

XX. A BED OF FIRE.

The sinner lies chained down on a bed of red-hot blazing fire! When a man, sick of fever, is lying on even a soft bed, it is pleasant sometimes to turn round. If the sick man lies on the same side for a long time, the skin comes off, the flesh gets raw. How will it be when the body has been lying on the same side on the scorching, broiling fire for a hundred millions of years! Now look at that body, lying on the bed of fire. All the body is salted with fire. The fire burns through every bone and every muscle. Every nerve is trembling and quivering with the sharp fire. The fire rages inside the skull, it shoots out through the eyes, it drops out through the ears, it roars in the throat as it roars up a chimney. So will mortal sin be punished. Yet there are people in their senses who commit mortal sin!

XXI. WORMS.

Isa. lxvi.—*"The worm that dieth not."* Judith xvi.—"He will give fire and worms into their flesh, that they may burn and feel for ever." St. Basil says that "in Hell there will be worms without number eating the flesh, and their bites will be unbearable." St. Teresa says that she found the entrance into Hell filled with these venomous insects. If you cannot bear the sight of ugly vermin and creeping things on the earth, will you be content with the sight of the venomous things in Hell, which are a million times worse? The bite or the pricking of one insect on the earth sometimes keeps you awake, and torments you for hours. How will you feel in Hell, when millions of them make their dwelling-place in your mouth, and ears, and eyes, and creep all over you, and sting you with their deadly stings through all eternity? You will not then be able to help yourself or send them away because you cannot stir hand or foot. One of the most painful things in the world is to be much frightened.

XXII. FRIGHT.

Wisd. xvii.—"While they thought to lie hid in their obscure sins, they were horribly afraid and troubled. For neither did the den which held them keep them from fear. For noises coming down troubled them, and sad visions appearing to them, affrighted them."

Do you know what is meant by being frightened out of one's senses? A boy wanted to frighten two other little boys. In the daytime he took some phosphorus, and marked with it the form of a skeleton on the wall of the room where the little boys always slept. In the daytime the mark of phosphorus is not seen; in the dark it shines like fire. The two little boys went to bed, knowing nothing about it. Next morning they opened the door of the room where the two little boys had been sleeping. They found one boy sitting on his bed, staring at the wall, out of his senses. The other little boy was lying dead! This was fright.

You will be lying helpless in the lonesome darkness of Hell. The devils come in the most frightful shapes on purpose to frighten you. Serpents come and hiss at you. Wild beasts come and roar at you. Death comes and stares at you. How would you feel, if at the dark hour of midnight, one that was dead should come to your bedside and stand over you and mock at you? You hear the most horrible shrieks and dismal sounds which you cannot understand. The sinner, frightened out of his senses at those terrible sighs in the darkness of Hell, roars out for help—but there is nobody to come and help him in his fright. Wisd. xvii.—*"Being scared with the passing of beasts and hissing of serpents, they died of fear."*

The greatest pain of Hell has not yet been told. You shall hear it now.

XXIII. THE PAIN OF LOSS.

It is easy to understand the other pains of Hell, because there are pains like them on earth. But it is difficult to understand the Pain of Loss, because there is nothing like it on earth. You must know that when a soul has been condemned to Hell at the judgment-seat, God lets it see for a moment something of what it has lost. It sees the immense happiness it would have had in Heaven with God and His angels and saints. And now it sees that all this blessed happiness is lost—lost by its own fault, lost for ever, lost without hope! Listen to the painful cry of a child which has lost its mother! Listen to the wailings of the people in Ireland when their sister is leaving them to go to America, and perhaps they will never see her any more. Then you may think what a wailing there will be when the soul hears these words from God: "Depart from Me for ever." Listen to the shriek of that madman shut up in the madhouse; he lost his money, his brain turned, and he became mad. Then you may think how the soul will shriek when it sees that it has lost Heaven. Listen to that splash in the river. A man threw himself off the bridge; as he was falling down into the river, he roared out: "I can bear death, but I cannot bear this loss." Listen to the tremendous roar at the judgment-seat. The soul dashes itself from the judgment-seat down into the flames of Hell, roaring out: "I can bear the fire of Hell, but I cannot bear the loss of Heaven *after I have seen what Heaven is*." Listen again to the devils in Hell, and you will hear them crying out: "I would gladly burn here for millions of years if I could only see God for one moment." Jer. xxiii.—*"In the latter days you shall understand these things."*

Now look to those little doors all round the walls of Hell. They are little rooms or dungeons where sinners are shut up. We will go and look at some of them.

XXIV. THE DUNGEONS OF HELL.

THE FIRST DUNGEON — A DRESS OF FIRE.

Job xxxviii.—*"Are not thy garments hot?"* Come into this room. You see it is very small. But see in the midst of it there is a girl, perhaps about eighteen years old. What a terrible dress she has on—her dress is made of fire. On her head she wears a bonnet of fire. It is pressed down close all over her head; it burns her head; it burns into the skin; it scorches the bone of the skull and makes it smoke. The red-hot fiery heat burns into the brain and melts it. Ezech. xxii.—"I will burn you in the fire of My wrath, you shall be *melted* in the midst thereof as silver is melted in the fire." You do not, perhaps, like a headache. Think what a headache that girl must have. But see more. She is wrapped up in flames, for her frock is fire. If she were on the earth she would be burnt to a cinder in a moment. But she is in Hell, where fire burns everything, but burns nothing away. There she stands burning and scorched; there she will stand for ever burning and scorched! She counts with her fingers the moments as they pass away slowly, for each moment seems to her like a hundred years. As she counts the moments she remembers that she will have to count them for ever and ever.

When that girl was alive she never thought about God or her soul. She cared only for one thing, and that was dress! Instead of going to Mass on Sundays, she went about the town and the parks to show off her dress. She disobeyed her father and mother by going to dancing houses and all kinds of bad places, to show off her dress. And now her dress is her punishment. *"For by what things a man sinneth, by the same also he is tormented."*— Wisd. xi.

XXV. THE SECOND DUNGEON.

THE DEEP PIT.

Luke xvi.—*"It came to pass that the rich man also died, and he was buried in the fire of Hell."* Think of a coffin not made of wood, but of fire, solid fire! And now come into this other room. You see a pit, a deep, almost bottomless, pit. Look down it and you will see something red-hot and burning. It is a coffin, a red-hot coffin of fire. A certain map is lying fastened in the inside of that coffin of fire. You might burst open a coffin made of iron; but that coffin made of solid fire never can be burst open. There that man lies and will lie for ever in the fiery coffin. It burns him from beneath. The sides of it scorch him. The heavy burning lid on the top presses down close upon him. The horrible heat in the inside chokes him; he pants for breath; he cannot breathe; he cannot bear it; he gets furious. He gathers up his knees and pushes out his hands against the top of the coffin to burst it open. His knees and hands are fearfully burned by the red-hot lid. No matter, to be choked is worse. He tries with all his strength to burst open the coffin. He cannot do it. He has no strength remaining. He gives it up and sinks down again. Again the horrible choking. Again he tries: again he sinks down; so he will go on for ever and ever! This man was very rich. Instead of worshipping God, he worshipped his money. Morning, noon, and night, he thought about nothing but his money. He was clothed in purple and fine linen. He feasted sumptuously every day. He was hard-hearted to the poor. He let a poor man die at his door, and would not even give him the crumbs that fell from his table. When he came into Hell the devil mocked him saying: *"What did pride profit you, or what advantage did the boasting of riches bring you? all those things have parsed away like a shadow."*—Wisd. v. Then the devil's sentence was that since he was so rich in the world, he should be very poor in Hell, and have nothing but a narrow, burning coffin.

XXVI. THE THIRD DUNGEON.

THE RED-HOT FLOOR.

Look into this room. What a dreadful place it is! The roof is red-hot; the walls are red-hot; the floor is like a thick sheet of red-hot iron. See, on the middle of that red-hot floor stands a girl. She looks about sixteen years old. Her feet are bare, she has neither shoes nor stockings on her feet; her bare feet stand on the red-hot burning floor. The door of this room has never been opened before since she first set her foot on the red-hot floor. Now she sees that the door is opening. She rushes forward. She has gone down on her knees on the red-hot floor. Listen! she speaks. She says: "I have been standing with my bare feet on this red-hot floor for years. Day and night my only standing-place has been this red-hot floor. Sleep never came on me for a moment, that I might forget this horrible burning floor. Look," she says, "at my burnt and bleeding feet. Let me go off this burning floor for one moment, only for one single, short moment. Oh, that in this endless eternity of years, I might forget the pain only for one single moment. "The devil answers her question: "Do you ask," he says, "for a moment, for one moment to forget your pain? No, not for one single moment during the never-ending eternity of years shall you ever leave this red-hot floor!" "Is it so?" the girl says with a sigh, that seems to break her heart; "then, at least, let somebody go to my little brothers and sisters who are alive, and tell them not to do the bad things which I did, so they will never have to come and stand on the red-hot floor." The devil answers her again: "Your little brothers and sisters have the priests to tell them these things. If they will not listen to the priests, neither would they listen, even if somebody should go to them from the dead."

Oh, that you could hear the horrible, the fearful scream of that girl when she saw the door shutting, never to be opened any more. The history of this girl is short. Her feet first led her into sin, so it is her feet which most of all are tormented. While yet a very little child, she began to go into bad company. The more she grew up, the more she went into bad company against the bidding of her parents. She used to walk about the streets at night, and do very wicked things. She died early. Her death was brought on by the bad life she led.

XXVII. THE FOURTH DUNGEON.

THE BOILING KETTLE.

Amos iv.—*"The days shall come when they shall lift you up on pikes, and what remains of you in boiling pots."* Look into this little prison. In the middle of it there is a boy, a young man. He is silent; despair is on him. He stands straight up. His eyes are burning like two burning coals. Two long flames come out of his ears. His breathing is difficult. Sometimes he opens his mouth, and breath of blazing fire rolls out of it. But listen! there is a sound just like that of a kettle boiling. Is it really a kettle which is boiling? No; then what is it? Hear what it is. The blood is boiling in the scalded veins of that boy. The brain is boiling and bubbling in his head. The marrow is boiling in his bones! Ask him, put the question to him, why is he thus tormented? His answer is, that when he was alive, his blood boiled to do very wicked things, and he did them, and it was for that he went to dancing-houses, public-houses and theatres. Ask him, does he think the punishment greater than he deserves? "No," he says, "my punishment is not greater than I deserve, it is just. I knew it not so well on earth, but I know now that it is just. There is a just and a terrible God. He is terrible to sinners in Hell—but He is just!"

XXVIII. THE FIFTH DUNGEON.

THE RED-HOT OVEN.

Ps. XX.—*"Thou shalt make him as an oven of fire in the time of Thy anger."* You are going to see again the child about which you read in the *Terrible Judgment*, that it was condemned to Hell. See! it is a pitiful sight. The little child is in this red-hot oven. Hear how it screams to come out. See how it turns and twists itself about in the fire. It beats its head against the roof of the oven. It stamps its little feet on the floor of the oven. You can see on the face of this little child what you see on the faces of all in Hell—despair, desperate and horrible!

The same law which is for others is also for children. If children, knowingly and willingly, break God's commandments, they also must be punished like others. This child committed very bad mortal sins, knowing well the harm of what it was doing, and knowing that Hell would be the punishment. God was very good to this child. Very likely God saw that this child would get worse and worse, and would never repent, and so it would have to be punished much more in Hell. So God in His mercy called it out of the world in its early childhood.

THE SIXTH DUNGEON.

A VOICE.

LISTEN at this door. Hear that voice; how sad and sorrowful it sounds. It says: "Oh, I am lost, I am lost. I am lost when I might have been saved. I am in Hell, and I might have been in Heaven. How short my sin, how long the punishment! besides I might have repented; I might have told that sin, but I was ashamed to confess it. Oh, the day on which I was born, I wish it had never been. Accursed be that day; but I am lost—lost—lost for ever — for ever—for ever." The voice dies away, and you hear it no more!

XXIX. HUNGER.

The prophet Isaias, chap, ix., says, that hunger will be so horrible, that every one shall eat the flesh of his own arm.

THE DRUNKARD.

Do you hear that man roaring out in the middle of Hell? How loud his voice is. It rises above all the groans, and shrieks, and cries, and screams, of millions. With a voice like thunder he roars out: "Oh, a drop of cold water, a drop of cold water to cool my tongue; my tongue is thirsty, my tongue is burning, my tongue is red-hot. Give me a drop of cold water, only one single drop of cold water to cool my burning tongue." The devil answers his roar with another roar: "You fool," he says, "you drunkard, why do you cry out for cold water to cool your burning tongue; there is no cold water in Hell." Still the drunkard goes on roaring for a drop of cold water. Now the devil lifts up a scourge of fire to strike him and make him hold his tongue. Then the drunkard sinks down into a deep pool of fire and brimstone, where he is drowned in destruction and perdition.

You drunkards, who on Saturday evenings are in the public-house, and on Sundays away from Mass; you drunkards, whose children are hungered and in rags, and go neither to Catechism nor Mass, go down to Hell, and listen to your brother-drunkard crying out for a drop of cold water to cool his burning tongue!

XXX. NO PEACE.

Job x.—*"A land of misery and darkness, where the shadow of death and no order, but everlasting horror dwelleth."*

See those children in dreadful anger beating their parents. They fly at them; they try to take life away from those who gave them life. "Cursed parents," they shout, "if you had not given us bad example, we should not now be in Hell." "Accursed father," cries a boy, "it was you that showed me the way to the public-house." "Accursed mother," cries a daughter, "it was you that taught me to love the world. You never warned me when I went into that company which was my ruin." "Cursed husband," cries that wife, "before I knew you I was good; I obeyed the laws of God. It was you that led me away from God, and made me break His laws. Like the devil you ruined my soul, and like the devil I will torment you for ever and ever." 1 Kings xxv.—*"When Nabal heard the words of his wife, his heart died within Aim, and he became as a stone."*

TWO VIPERS.

DID you ever see two deadly vipers fly at each other? Their eyes burning with rage. They shoot out their poisoned stings. They struggle to give each other the death-blow. They struggle till they have torn the flesh and blood from each other. You may see the like of this in Hell. See that young man and young woman—how changed they are. They loved each other so much on earth, that for this they broke the laws of God and man. But now they fight each other like two vipers, and so they will fight for all eternity.

Hellmouth from *Hours of Catherine of Cleves*,
by the Master of Catherine of Cleves, circa 1440.
(Morgan Library & Museum,
Public Domain/Wikimedia Commons)

A PICTURE OF HELL.

There was a glass which made things look three million times larger than they really are. A drop of dirty water was looked at through this glass. Millions of frightful little insects were seen in the water. These insects seemed to be always fighting and beating and trying to kill each other. They gave themselves no rest. It was always fighting, beating—beating, fighting. Sometimes thousands would throw themselves on other thousands and swallow them up alive. Sometimes they tore away pieces from each other's bodies, which still remained alive, only looking more frightful than before. Such is Hell!

XXXI. ETERNITY.

Matt. xxv.—*"These shall go into everlasting punishment."*

There is one thing which could change Hell into Heaven. An angel of God comes to the gates of Hell and says, "Listen to me, all ye people in Hell, for I bring you good news. You will still burn in Hell for almost countless millions of years. But a day will come, and on that day the pains of Hell will be no more! You will go out of Hell." If such a message came, Hell would no longer be Hell. Hell would no longer be a house of blasphemy, but a house of prayer and thanksgiving and joy. But such a message will never come to Hell, because God has said that the punishment of Hell shall be everlasting.

THE QUESTION.

You say what is meant by everlasting. It is both easy and difficult to answer this question. It is easy to say that the pains of Hell will last for ever, and never have an end.

It is difficult to answer the question, because our understandings are too little to understand what is meant by the word *ever*. We know very well what is meant by a year, a million of years, a hundred million of years. But for ever—Eternity—What is that?

A MEASURE—A BIRD.

We can measure almost anything. We can measure a field or a road. We can measure the earth. We can measure how far it is from the earth to the sun. Only one thing there is which never has been and never will be measured, and that is Eternity—for ever!

Think of a great solid iron ball, larger than the Heavens and the earth. A bird comes once in a hundred millions of years and just touches the great iron ball with a feather of its wing. Think that you have to burn in a fire till the bird has worn the great iron ball away with its feather. Is this Eternity? No.

XXXII. TEARS. — SAND. — DOTS.

Think that a man in Hell cries only one single tear in ten hundred millions of years. Tell me how many millions of years must pass before he fills a little basin with his tears? how many millions of years must pass before he cries as many tears as there were drops of water at the deluge? how many years must pass before he has drowned the heavens and earth with his tears? Is this Eternity? No.

Turn all the earth into little grains of sand, and fill all the skies and the heavens with little grains of sand. After each hundred millions of years, one grain of sand is taken away; oh what a long, long time it would be before the last grain of sand was taken away. Is this Eternity? No.

Cover all the earth and all the skies with little dots like these . . . Let every dot stand for a hundred thousand millions of years. Is this Eternity? No.

After such a long, long time will God still punish sinners? Yes. Isa. ix.—*"After all this His anger is not turned away, His hand is still stretched out."* How long, then, will the punishment of sinners go on? For ever, and ever, and ever!

XXXIII. WHAT ARE THEY DOING?

PERHAPS at this moment, seven o'clock in the evening, a child is just going into Hell. To-morrow evening at seven o'clock, go and knock at the gates of Hell, and ask what the child is doing. The devils will go and look. Then they will come back again and say, *the child is burning!* Go in a week and ask what the child is doing; you will get the same answer—*it is burning!* Go in a year and ask; the same answer comes—*it is burning!* Go in a million of years and ask the same question; the answer is just the same—*it is burning!* So if you go for ever and ever, you will always get the same answer—*it is burning in the fire!*

WHAT O'CLOCK—THE DISMAL SOUND.

LOOK at that deep pool of fire and brimstone. See, a man has just lifted his head up out of it. He wants to ask a question. He speaks to a devil who is standing near him. He says: "What a long, long time it seems since I first came into Hell; I have been sunk down in this deep pool of burning fire. Years and years have passed away. I kept no count of time. Tell me then what o'clock is it?" "You fool," the devil answers, "why do you ask what o'clock it is? there is no clock in Hell; a clock is to tell the time with. But in Hell time is no more. It is Eternity!" Ps. lxxx.—*"Their time shall be for ever."*

Perhaps on a dark lonesome night you may have seen something waving backwards and forwards in the air. The sound of it was sad and mournful. It frightened you although it was but the branch of a tree.

Such a sound there is in Hell. It passes on without stopping from one end of Hell to the other. As it comes sweeping past, you hear it. What then is this dismal sound? It is the sound of Eternity—ever!—never!

XXXIV. TOO LATE!

LET us ask one of those souls scorched in the flames of Hell, to come and kneel before the Cross and see if its sins can be forgiven, and if it may come out of Hell. "Poor soul, then burning in the unquenchable fire of Hell, come and kneel before the Cross of Christ, and ask Him for pardon."

See now that soul is kneeling before the Cross.

THE PRAYER OF A LOST SOUL.

THIS lost soul says: "O Christ, I am tormented in this flame. Day and night the tears run down from my eyes, like torrents. Christ, you were my Creator; you redeemed me; you are a merciful God. I come before you to ask if I may go out of this terrible fire where I am tormented."

THE ANSWER OF JESUS CHRIST.

"UNHAPPY soul!" Jesus says; "I have pity for you, because, indeed, I was your Creator, and I did not create you for pain but for happiness. I wished you to be in Heaven and not in Hell. How could I wish you to be in Hell, seeing what I did to save you from Hell? Remember how I came down from Heaven to the very earth to save you from Hell. Do you remember how I was mocked and spit upon, and pierced with thorns; I was nailed to the wood of the Cross, and died in shame and cruel agony. What was all this for? It was for you, to save you from Hell. And if this is not enough, I will tell you, that from all eternity I was thinking how to save you, and My heart was thirsting to save you. I cared for your happiness more than for My own, for I left My own happiness in Heaven and went down to the earth to be tormented for your sake. When My Father, who is in Heaven, had seen what I had done for you, He said, 'Surely I will give that soul all the graces it needs, and thousand times more than it needs, to save itself.'

"Then the days of your life came. You were not made like the beasts of the field. You had sense and understanding to know that it is right to do good and wrong to do evil. Besides, I said to you: *Do good and you shall he happy for ever in Heaven; but if you do evil you shall he punished for ever in Hell.* I wrote this on your heart. You heard it with your ears thousands of times during your life. You knew, you felt that what I said was right and just. If on earth a man deserves punishment who breaks a law of one who is only a man, how much more does he deserve punishment who breaks the law made by Me, his Creator and his God.'

"Then you, knowing full well that Hell would be the punishment, did evil. You broke My Commandments. Then I might in justice have sent you to Hell. But I did not. I had pity on you; I warned you to repent. I told you repentance was easy. Instead of repenting you broke My laws again, and again and again. You went on breaking My law. I went on asking, begging of you to repent. In the anguish of My heart I asked you to save your soul from everlasting punishment. But you despised all My counsels, you neglected My reprehensions, you treated Me most ungratefully as you would not have done to any man on the earth. You seemed to be weary of My kindness. But I who knew what punishment was coming upon you, was not weary with trying to save you from it.

"The days fixed for your life were coming to an end. A thousand times I brought to your remembrance that death which was coming swiftly. You did not care. The last moment of your life came and nothing had been done. You had done everything *except the one great thing—to try to save your soul*. If you had only taken a little of that trouble to save your soul which you threw away on a thousand trifling things, your soul would have been saved. Death came. You stood before My judgment-seat. You were condemned to the eternal punishments of Hell. You confessed that My sentence was just. You could not deny it. And now you come and ask Me to change the everlasting sentence, and let you go out of Hell. I promised eternal happiness to those who do good, punishment in Hell to those who do evil. I must keep My promise—I cannot break it. It was a mercy that the punishment of Hell was made everlasting. If so many broke My law, knowing that the punishment would be everlasting, how would it have been, if the punishment had not been everlasting? There are millions in Heaven who would not have been there but for the everlasting pains of Hell. They were wise; they thought on the eternal years of punishment. You could have done the same, but you would not. Besides, even now sin is in your heart as it was when you died. You hate the punishment, but not the sin; your heart is ready to break My law again, and so it will be for ever.

"Unhappy soul! you ask now for mercy; but it is too late. If you had asked for mercy when you were alive, how glad I should have been to be merciful to you. But now it is too late to ask for mercy. You must go back into everlasting punishment."

The sinner knows and feels that a wrong thing would be done if he were set free from eternal punishment. So he goes back into the flames of Hell hopeless and desperate.

XXXV. DESPAIR.

Jer. xlvi.—*"There is no cure for thee."*

Let us look at Hell once more before we leave it. See that man who just asked for mercy and could not get it. He cannot bear the scorching fire which burns his body through and through. But he must bear it. On the earth the hungry man looks for bread, and at last he gets it. A sick man looks for his pain to get less, and at last it gets less. The man in Hell looks for the burning to stop—but it does not stop. Then he begins to think how long will the horrible burning go on. His thoughts go through millions and millions of years that cannot be counted. Will the burning stop then? His understanding tells him, No—never—never—never!

See in his agony of despair he has thrown himself on his knees. He prays! he prays with his eyes and hands lifted up. O how well he prays; no distraction comes to take his thoughts off his prayer. To whom does he pray?

Does he pray to God? No prayer ever goes up from Hell to God. *"For there is no tongue that shall confess to Thee, O God, in Hell."*—Ps. vi. To whom then does he pray? He prays to Death! "O Death," he says, "come and put me out of this horrible pain. O Death, when I was alive I feared you; I kept away from you. But now, Death, I love you. O Death, be kind to me; come and kill me. "Does Death come? No! Death flies away from him. *"In those days men shall seek death and shall not find it."*—Apoc. ix.

He finds that his prayer is not heard. He stoops down; he takes up two great handsful of fire; he throws the fire down his throat to kill himself. *"He looks for death and it Cometh not."*—Job iii. He is on his feet again; he runs like a madman towards the walls of Hell. He dashes his head up against the walls. He hopes that his brains will be beaten out, and that he will die, and that his torments will end. *"He looks for death and it cometh not."*

THE KNIFE.

SEE that great strong man. He rushes furiously through Hell. As he goes along, he splashes the fire and sulphur about him with his feet. Those who are in his road fly away in terror. He bellows out like a mad bull; he says: "Bring me the knife—bring me the knife." He was a murderer. He killed somebody with a knife. Now he wants to get the knife, and kill himself with it. Sometimes he thrusts out his hand as if to catch at the knife; but he is deceived. The knife is not there; *he looks for death and it cometh not.*

XXXVI. THE VISION OF ST. TERESA.

St. Teresa writes: "One day when I was praying, it seemed to me that suddenly, in one moment, I found myself in Hell. I did not know how I came there. Only I understood that our Lord wanted me to see the place which the devil had prepared for me. I was in Hell for a very short time; but if I was to live for many years I could never forget it.

"The entrance into Hell seemed to me like a long narrow passage or a low dark oven. The floor was very filthy, and the smell which came from it was abominable. Great numbers of venomous insects were creeping about it. At the end of this passage there was a wall with a kind of hole or cupboard in it. I found myself all at once squeezed into this place. What I had seen in the narrow passage was most frightful. Yet it might be called even pleasant compared with the torments of the place into which I had been squeezed. These torments were so terrible, that I cannot give any account of the least part of them. I found my soul burning in such a horrible fire, that I could not make anybody understand it. During my illnesses I have felt the most dreadful pains which the doctors tell us can be felt in this world. But all these pains are nothing—nothing like the pains I felt in Hell. Then there was the horror I felt when I thought that these pains would never come to an end, but would last for ever. I felt as if I was always at every moment strangled and choked. It seemed as if some one was always tearing my soul in pieces, or rather as if my soul was always tearing itself in pieces. I felt myself always burning, and as if I was being cut, and broken and crushed in pieces. In this most frightful place there was not the least hope of any relief. It was impossible either to sit or lie down, for there is no room to sit or lie down. The very walls are most frightful, and seem to close on you and strangle you. There was not the least light there, but only the thickest and blackest darkness. Yet somehow or other, I know not how, you see there whatever is dreadful and terrible. God did not allow me to see more of Hell at that time. But afterwards He let me see other much more frightful torments for particular sins. I could not understand in what manner these things were seen by me. But I understood that God did me a very great favour in letting me see those terrible torments from which He had saved me. All I have read or heard about Hell is as different from the real pains of Hell as a picture is different from the thing painted. To be burnt in the fire of this world is a mere nothing, a trifle if compared with being burnt in Hell. It is now six years since I saw Hell. Yet even now I cannot write about it without feeling my blood frozen with horror. When I think about the pains of Hell, all the pains of this world seem to me not worth thinking about. It seems to me that we have no reason to complain about the pains of this life. I look upon it as one of the greatest graces of God to have seen the pains of Hell. It takes away all fear of the pains of this life. It makes us suffer them patiently, and thank God in the hope that He will deliver us from the terrible pains of Hell, which will last for ever! Since I had this vision, there are no pains which it does not seem to me easy to bear, remembering what I saw in Hell. I often wonder I could before read of the pains of Hell, and not be frightened by them, or how I could find pleasure in those things which lead to Hell. 'O my God, be Thou for ever blessed. You have shown me that You love me more than I love myself, by delivering me so often from that frightful prison, into which I was so ready to enter against Your will.' The sight of Hell has made me feel immense pain when I think of those heretics and bad Catholics who are lost. My desire to see them saved from these pains is so immense that I would willingly give a thousand lives, if I had them, to save one of these souls."

A PAIR OF SCALES.

IF you want to know the weight of some sugar, you get a pair of scales. You put the sugar into one scale and a weight into the other. If you want to know the badness of mortal sin, put it into one scale, and pains of Hell into another scale. You will see that the balance stands equal. *A mortal sin of out moment deserves the everlasting pains of Hell.*

THE PAST; OR, BREAK THE EGG.

YOU only see the outside of an egg. If you knew that there was some frightful venomous creature hatching in the egg, you would break it in pieces, directly. Mortal sin is an egg which the devil puts in your soul, if you let him. You only see the outside of the devil's egg. In the inside there is the most horrible and abominable monster that ever was. He who dies with this diabolic egg in his soul, will burn in the flames of Hell for ever and ever.

If you have committed a mortal sin, you know that the diabolic egg is in your soul. Break that frightful egg in pieces. Break it before you lay down this book. Break it before you stir hand or foot; break it *this very moment*. If you wait till the next moment you may be in Hell the next moment! How must you break this diabolic egg? Make an Act of Contrition for your sin. If God sees that your Act of Contrition is sincere. He will forgive you *directly*. But then you must go to Confession as soon as you can and confess it.

An Act of Contrition.—*O my God, I am very sorry that I have sinned against You, because You are so good, and I will not sin again.*

THE FUTURE; OR, THE DEVIL'S TRAP.

Temptation, especially bad company, is the devil's trap by which he brings you into mortal sin. Keep away from temptation when you know of it before. Fly away if it comes when you are not expecting it, and say—Jesus and Mary, help me.

Remember! if you die in mortal sin you burn In the flames of Hell for all eternity. You understand this quite well. So if you have the misfortune to go to Hell, you will have no one to blame but yourself.

XXXVII. THE VISION IN VEN. BEDE.

"A certain man," says Ven. Bede, "fell sick, and died in the beginning of the night. Next morning early he suddenly came to life again, and sat up. He told the people what he had seen. 'I was led,' he said, 'into a dark place. When I came into it, the darkness grew so thick that I could see nothing but the form of him who led me. I saw a great many balls of black fire rising up out of a deep pit and falling back again. I saw that there were souls shut up in these balls of fire. The smell which came out of the pit was unbearable. He who led me into this place went away. So I stood there in great fright, not knowing what to do. All at once I heard behind me voices crying and lamenting most fearfully. I heard other voices mocking and laughing. These voices came nearer and nearer to me, and grew louder and louder. Then I saw that those who were laughing and rejoicing were devils. These devils were dragging along with them souls of men which were howling and lamenting. Amongst them I saw a man and a woman. The devils dragged these souls down into the burning pit. When they had gone deep down into the pit, I could not hear their voices so well. After a while some of these dark spirits came up again from the flaming pit. They ran forward and came round me. I was terribly frightened by their flaming eyes, and the stinking fire which came out of their mouths and nostrils. They seemed as if they would lay hold of me with burning tongs which they held in their hands. I looked around me for help. Just then I saw something like a star shining in the darkness. The light came from him who had brought me into this place. When he came near, the devils went away.' Then he said: 'That fiery, stinking pit which you saw is the mouth of Hell, and whosoever goes into it shall never come out again. Go back to your body and live among men again. Examine your actions well, and speak and behave so that you may be with the blessed in heaven.' When he had said this, on a sudden I found myself alive again amongst men."

THE END.

Hell. Engraving after Buonamico di Martino called Buffalmacco,
Circa 1480-1489. (Wellcome Collection)

ALSO FROM
CURIOUS PUBLICATIONS

The Embalmed Head of Oliver Cromwell: A Memoir
by Marc Hartzman

Psycho-Phone Messages
by Francis Grierson

*Spectropia, or Surprising Spectral Illusions Showing Ghosts
Everywhere*
by J. H. Brown

Spirit Slate Writing and Kindred Phenomena
by William E. Robinson

*The Talking Dead: A Collection of Messages
from Beyond the Veil, 1850s to 1920s*
Edited by Marc Hartzman

How to Speak With the Dead: A Practical Handbook
by Sciens

curiouspublications.com

CPSIA information can be obtained
at www.ICGtesting.com
Printed in the USA
BVHW030749080621
609004BV00005B/88

9 780986 239397